Why Do We Wear?

Uniforms
through History

by
Fiona MacDonald

GARETH STEVENS
GS
PUBLISHING
A Member of the WRC Media Family of Companies

Please visit our Web site at: www.garethstevens.com
For a free color catalog describing Gareth Stevens Publishing's
list of high-quality books and multimedia programs, call
1-800-542-2595 (USA) or 1-800-387-3178 (Canada).
Gareth Stevens Publishing's fax: (414) 332-3567.

Library of Congress Cataloging-in-Publication Data available upon request from publisher.
Fax (414) 336-0157 for the attention of the Publishing Records Department.

ISBN-10: 0-8368-6858-7 — ISBN-13: 978-0-8368-6858-6 (lib. bdg.)

This North American edition first published in 2007 by
Gareth Stevens Publishing
A Member of the WRC Media Family of Companies
330 West Olive Street, Suite 100
Milwaukee, Wisconsin 53212 USA

This edition copyright © 2007 by Gareth Stevens, Inc. Original edition copyright © 2006
by ticktock Entertainment Ltd. First published in Great Britain by ticktock Media Ltd.,
Unit 2 Orchard Business Centre, North Farm Road, Tunbridge Wells, Kent TN2 3XF.

Managing editor: Valerie J. Weber
Gareth Stevens editor: Gini Holland
Gareth Stevens art direction: Tammy West
Gareth Stevens designer: Kami Strunsee

Picture Credits (t=top, b=bottom, l=left, r=right, c=center)
Bridgeman Art Library; 6-7 all, 16 all, 21 all; CORBIS: cover, 4 all, 14-15c, 15t, 17 all, 26t, 26b, 27t, 28-29 all;
Shutterstock: 15b; South American Pictures: 18-19 all; Superstock: 5t; ticktock Media Image Archive: 5b, 12-13 all,
20 all, 22-23 all, 24-25 all, 27 b; Werner Forman Archive: 8-9 all, 10-11 all

Every effort has been made to trace the copyright holders, and we apologize in advance for any unintentional omission.
We would be pleased to insert the appropriate acknowledgements in any subsequent edition of this publication.

Printed in the United States of America

1 2 3 4 5 6 7 8 9 10 09 08 07 06

Table of Contents

Cover: In Great Britain, a Yeoman of the Guard still wears a uniform based
on Tudor designs.

Words that appear in the glossary are printed in
boldface type the first time they occur in the text.

Introduction

Uniforms can make us feel proud of our classmates, our sports teams, and our school.

Originally, the word *uniform* was just a way of describing things that all looked or felt the same. Today, *uniform* is mostly used as the name for a type of clothing. Uniforms must be made in a specific color or design and be worn by many people for the same purpose.

Signs of Belonging

Some uniforms are cheap and simple. Others are costly and elaborate. They may be home-made, purchased, or given to wearers by the people they work for. Uniforms show that the wearer belongs to one special group — such as a school, an army, a profession, or a band — or a thousand other types of organizations. Uniforms often help people feel they belong together because their clothes look alike.

A Sense of Tradition

Many uniforms feature traditional garments or symbolic colors. They may date from a time when the group that first wore them achieved great success or won famous victories. Uniforms can also symbolize values — such as courage and team spirit — that leaders wish to encourage today. They can stand for political ideas or political beliefs that organizations wish to protect or preserve.

This evzone (guard) on duty in Greece is wearing a dress uniform, which is for special occasions, based on **tunics** and jackets worn by famous Greek freedom fighters 500 years ago.

Great Expectations

Uniforms can change the way we behave. They represent the qualities we expect to find in the people who wear them. We usually trust uniformed nurses and expect them to be kind. We fight against — or flee from — soldiers wearing enemy uniforms. Sometimes rebels choose to wear some uniform items, such as hats or jackets. These identify them to their enemies — but also to their comrades, so that they do not accidentally attack each other in battle.

The familiar white coat of this vet instantly identifies the wearer as a medical professional and offers reassurance to the owner of the dog he is examining.

Professional Pride

Many uniforms are linked to professions and occupations. They are designed to be practical and, if need be, protective, such as the tough overalls worn by engineering workers or the waterproof jackets and pants worn by motorcycle police. Uniforms also help create a favorable image of each profession. Orchestral musicians wear dark colored but glamorous evening clothes. Executives from multinational companies usually choose smart, sober, tailored suits to show that they are serious about their work.

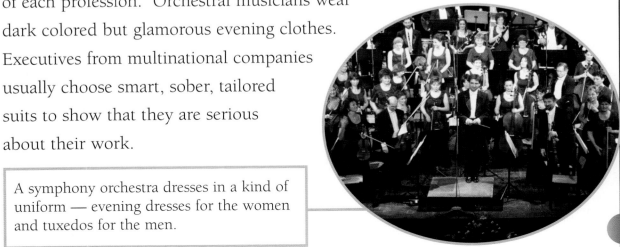

A symphony orchestra dresses in a kind of uniform — evening dresses for the women and tuxedos for the men.

The First Uniforms

Clothes made in true uniform style are a fairly new invention given the long history of people on Earth. The first official uniforms were made about 2,000 years ago. For many centuries before then, people put on special clothes, jewels, and make-up to show their identity and group membership.

Dancing Together

Few examples of prehistoric uniforms have survived until today. Some ancient styles are preserved by people who still practice traditional arts, such as dancing. Their clothes show the dance's purpose, such as a coming-of-age ritual. In war dances, warriors wore body paint to show their **rank** and bravery. In some religious rituals, dancers dressed in the same way to confuse evil spirits who might attack one of the dancers.

Maori men and women from New Zealand perform a traditional dance.

Ghost Dancers

Some uniforms were believed to have magical powers. They might be made of special materials such as certain animal skins or decorated with **talismans** (objects with supposed magical powers). Belief in these uniforms continued for thousands of years. In the nineteenth century, for example, Native Americans fighting against European settlers joined a religious movement known as the

This Ghost Dance shirt was made of fringed deer skin decorated with birds and stars.

Ghost Dance Society. Members wore special shirts that were said to have supernatural powers.

Larger than Life

Many traditional uniforms were designed to terrify enemies by making the men who wore them seem larger than life. Feather warbonnets, worn in many parts of North and South America, increased the wearer's height by up to 1.6 feet (.5 meter). In southern Africa, Zulu soldiers wore headdresses made from lions' manes. As well as increasing height, this headdress also suggested that Zulu men shared the power and strength of "the king of the beasts." Headdresses are still worn in ceremonies today.

This Zulu warrior from South Africa was photographed in about 1890.

Healers Set Apart

In many past societies, **shamans** (healers) believed they could get help from the gods by drumming, fasting, or taking herbal potions. For these healing rituals, shamans put on special clothes or masks. This "uniform" set them apart from ordinary people and allowed them to behave in unusual ways. Today, doctors do not claim to heal with magic, but their white uniforms send out a similar message. They suggest that doctors are special people who act in a trained, professional manner. They make it all right for doctors to do things, such as examine patients, that other people would not be allowed to do.

What happened to the Ghost Dancers?

A Blackfoot shaman wears an animal mask and skins.

Ancient Egypt and Its Neighbors

The hot, dry climate of North Africa meant that most ancient Egyptians wore very few clothes. In spite of this, the differences between their garments were extremely important. Each item of Egyptian clothing, headgear, and jewelry displayed its wearer's wealth, rank, or occupation.

Royal Symbols

The Egyptians believed that their pharaohs, or kings, were not just ordinary rulers. They thought they were superhuman. As a sign of their power, pharaohs wore crowns or a special striped *nemes* headdress and carried a **crook** (hooked stick) and a **flail** (a heavy rod). The crook was used by shepherds to rescue sheep, so it was a sign of the pharaoh's care for his people. The flail was used for threshing grain, so it represented strength and fertility.

A wall painting shows an Egyptian pharaoh carrying a crook and flail and dressed in a striped headdress.

Pure and Holy

Pharaohs and their senior wives had many religious duties. They shared these with priests and priestesses recruited from noble Egyptian families. Before taking part in religious rituals, priests and priestesses had to be pure. They washed all over and shaved all the hair from their heads and bodies. They dressed in clean white **kilts** or **tunics**, woven from linen. Wool and leather were thought to be unclean. The only animal products permitted were beautiful, valuable leopard skins, worn by high-ranking priests and priestesses.

A senior priestess, draped in leopard skin, sits on a stool carved with animal feet and a decorative tail.

These fly-shaped medals, which were awarded for valor, are made of real gold.

For Valor

Egypt was defended on all sides by natural barriers — deserts, **cataracts** (waterfalls) on the Nile River, and the sea. All able-bodied Egyptian men had a duty to serve in the pharaoh's army. They wore their own clothes and supplied their own weapons, but, if they fought well, they might be rewarded by the pharaoh with eye-catching medals. Shaped liked flies, these medals told onlookers that the wearer had bravely "bitten" or "stung" the enemy and deserved honor.

Battle Technology

In neighboring lands close to Egypt, **Mesopotamian** peoples were famous for pioneering new ways of fighting. By about 2500 B.C., they had invented the first-known padded metal helmets and the earliest armored clothing. At first, soldiers wore leather cloaks covered with domed discs of hammered metal. Later, they replaced the discs with overlapping metal plates sewn onto tunics made of leather. After about 1500 B.C., Assyrians began to wear hobnailed boots for fighting rather than open-toed sandals. All these special garments gave soldiers an advantage over their enemies. They also acted like a national uniform, making them instantly recognizable.

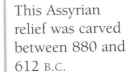

This Assyrian relief was carved between 880 and 612 B.C.

9

Ancient Greece and Rome

A ncient Greece was divided into hundreds of **city-states.** They did not share one single Greek style of dress because each Greek city-state was loyal to its own ancient customs and traditions. These customs formed the basis of distinctive local uniforms in clothing, weapons, and styles of armor.

In the city-state of Sparta, slave soldiers always wore red tunics.

Written Symbols

Each Greek city-state was defended by an army of **hoplites** (foot soldiers) and cavalry. Men from the same state all wore similar armor. For example, in Sparta, officers' helmets usually had a crest running sideways over the head from ear to ear. Elsewhere, Greek crests ran from front to back.

Ancient Rome

Uniforms are often a sign of a strong, central government. Between about 100 B.C. and A.D. 400, the Romans ruled the mightiest empire the world had yet seen. Roman troops were some of the first to wear a simple kind of uniform.

Army Issue

The earliest Roman soldiers were all Roman citizens. At first, they wore their own local clothes. Later, these were provided by army officers and based on

A Roman officer from about A.D. 150 wears a typical Roman tunic, helmet, and metal armor, plus short pants copied from the regular soldiers' styles.

standard (or "uniform") designs. As a sign of rank, Roman officers wore red cloaks and had horsehair crests on their helmets. After about 100 B.C., the Roman Empire grew rapidly, and the Romans began to recruit soldiers from conquered lands. Each legion wore its own local clothes, such as Celtic pants, or tight-fitting caps from Gaul (now France and Belgium). In the first and second centuries A.D., deadly fights between gladiators were very popular in Rome. Fighters dressed in different uniforms. A heavily armored man usually fought against a less well-protected one.

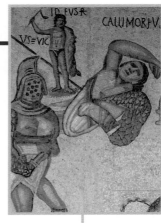

Roman gladiators wore shoulder protectors.

Toga-wearing politicians, illustrated here, served in the Roman **senate**.

c 500 B.C. – 200 B.C.

For Citizens Only

The toga was the usual clothing worn by Roman men. Togas are large, semi-circular cloaks that were made of natural beige or white wool and draped around the body. Foreigners and slaves were not allowed to wear them. Emperors' togas were purple. Politicians running for office had their togas washed in a special whitener. They became known as "**candidates**" (Latin for "white-robed").

Covering Up

Roman men and women used a fold of their tunics to cover their heads when making offerings to the gods. Priests and priestesses wore an extra veil. It symbolized holiness, purity, and respect for the gods, and it was draped over the back of the head, neck, and shoulders.

A vestal virgin priestess wears a headband in her hair plus a long veil over her shoulders.

Medieval Europe

In early medieval Europe, people did not wear official uniforms. Then, between A.D. 1000 and A.D. 1500, changes in the Catholic Church — and also new ways of fighting — led to the development of many specially designed clothes.

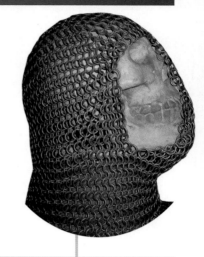

Chain mail was supposed to protect the wearer from sword blows, but it was very awkward to wear.

Fighting Mad

Members of armies were among the first people to wear real uniforms. Among the Vikings of Scandinavia, extremely savage warriors wore tunics made of bearskin. Known as **Berserkers** (bear shirts), they worked themselves up into a fury, shouting, stamping, and chewing their shields. In the early medieval era, most warriors wore **chain mail**. Then, **plate armor** (personal armor made from large metal plates) replaced chain mail to cover the chest and sometimes the entire body.

This fifteenth-century painting features the heraldic shields of the von Esendorf family.

Heraldry

It was difficult for soldiers wearing armor to look from side to side or to turn round quickly. To help recognize friends — and foes — in battle, medieval fighting men painted patterns on their shields and **surcoats** (loose cloth robes worn on top of armor). Each noble family had its own design, which was also worn by its followers like a uniform. Royal servants learned all the different designs and organized them into a new picture language, called "heraldry." Even today, some people know their families' heraldry.

These Göss Vestments, made in the thirteenth century for priests, feature squares with beautifully embroidered pictures of birds and mythical beasts.

Holy Habits

The Catholic church was the most powerful organization in medieval Europe because even kings and queens had to obey its rules. Its influence spread throughout Europe. It encouraged many believers to live apart from the world in communities of monks and nuns. To show that they were dedicated to God, monks and nuns wore dark, drab uniforms called **habits**. Ordinary priests and church leaders also wore long, dark garments. When taking part in church services, they added boldly colored vestments (holy robes). These included miters (hats), stoles (scarves), and copes (cloaks).

What uniform did medieval Christians wear to show they were sorry for their sins?

Professional Costumes

Most medieval men and women were peasants who made a living from farming. Their clothes were plain, simple, and usually homemade. Toward the end of the medieval era, new groups of professional people began to train and work in Europe. These ranged from doctors, lawyers, and professors to singers, dancers, and jesters (clowns). Most had their own special uniforms. Learned men wore dark robes similar to monks' habits. Entertainers wore amazing costumes in bright, contrasting colors.

A fourteenth-century illustration shows a doctor about to perform an eye operation.

Asia has been home to many different civilizations, each with different customs and traditions. Local political, economic, and environmental conditions have influenced all Asian uniforms, however. Some uniforms are only worn locally. Most uniforms are for military or ceremonial wear.

Religious Robes

Buddhism was founded by an Indian prince called Gautama Siddhartha. After meditating, he came to believe that humans could only find happiness by giving up earthly passions, such as greed and envy. Followers called him Buddha, which means "the enlightened one." To symbolize their devotion to Buddha's ideas and to show they are monks, Buddhist monks shave their heads and wear simple saffron-colored (orange) robes.

Buddhist monks wear orange.

Guarding the Emperor

Chinese warrior prince Zheng was the first ruler to unite the separate, warring states of China. He founded the first Chinese empire and took a new title, Qin Shi Huangdi (All-Powerful Chinese Emperor). He recruited a new army; introduced new laws, coins, weights, and measures; and employed a new civil service. When he died, his body was buried in a magnificent tomb. Thousands of lifelike terra-cotta warriors were buried close by to guard his spirit. These clay figures show us what his army's uniforms looked like.

Terra-cotta warriors at Qin's tomb show the uniforms of his army.

Muslim Sufi dancers, called dervishes, wear long kaftans and tall, domed hats.

Whirling Dervishes

The faith of Islam was founded by the Prophet Muhammad, who died in A.D. 632. Since the religion's early days, one of the more unusual ways of practicing Islam has been Sufi mysticism, which uses meditation, chanting, and holy dervish dancing to try to reach God. The long woolen robes that Sufis wear are called *sufs*. They are made to look like robes that the Prophet Muhammad wore during one of his journeys. When Sufis whirl, their robes spin in wide circles around their bodies, making beautiful patterns as they dance.

Entertaining Costumes

Throughout Asia, some women and men worked hard to entertain others. Some were actors, musicians, or temple dancers. For all these roles, performers put on clothes that were often just like uniforms. For example, in Japan, a specially chosen few women trained as geishas (elegant entertainers). If people saw women with white face makeup and elegant kimonos, they knew they were geishas. Geishas also took part in religious and political rituals.

Two modern geishas dress in their distinctive costumes and white makeup.

Who else was buried with emperor Qin Shi Huangdi?

Africa

Africa is a vast continent with many different languages, cultures, and traditions. In the past, formal uniforms were rare in Africa. Top soldiers often wore similar clothing to their comrades, and ordinary soldiers throughout Africa relied on traditional beliefs, rather than specialized clothes, for protection.

The "Honor of Trousers"

The kingdom of Mali, in northwest Africa, controlled a wide empire. Mali's greatest ruler was King Mansa Musa (reigned 1312–1337). His troops fought on horseback and on foot. Cavalrymen dressed in metal helmets, spiked collars, and breastplates covered by cotton robes. To reward brave, successful soldiers, rulers of Mali created the "Honor of the Trousers," handing over splendid garments for each courageous deed or victory. The soldiers who wore the largest number of trousers at once could easily be recognized as the bravest and the best.

A modern illustration shows King Mansa Musa, King of Mali.

These warriors belonged to the Leopard Hunters' Guild.

Animal Power

The kingdom of Benin (now part of Nigeria) was powerful between about 1400 and 1700. Its top warriors belonged to a secret brotherhood called the Leopard Hunters' Guild. In battle, they wore uniform helmets and armor made from a most unusual material — tough, scaly anteater skin. Anteaters are one of the few creatures that can survive being attacked by leopards. By wearing anteater skins, Benin warriors got protection from both leopard attacks and human enemies.

16

Magical Protection

Ordinary soldiers throughout Africa could rarely afford fine uniforms made from valuable animal skins. They usually went into battle naked or dressed in everyday clothes. These ranged from wrapped cloth garments to brief leather aprons or simple tunics woven from tough, fibrous plants. In central Africa, for example, warriors in Kongo (now the Democratic Republic of the Congo) made uniforms out of palm leaves. Instead of uniforms and armor, many African soldiers trusted in fetishes (magic amulets) for safety and used bells and rattles to summon helpful spirits or drive evil ghosts away.

This elaborate Kongo fetish was used to scare evil spirits away.

Islamic Influences

The faith of Islam reached North Africa between A.D. 700 and 800. It spread slowly to other parts of the continent, carried by soldiers and traders. In many parts of Africa, colors had important symbolic meanings. West African Muslims, in particular, believed that white is the color of joy. They wore white clothes on Fridays, the Muslim holy day, when believers rest from work and go to mosques to listen to preachers and pray alongside fellow members of their community.

This nineteenth-century photograph shows a Muslim from Ghana in a traditional uniform.

What uniform was given to dead people?

Early Americas

The many different peoples living in North and South America each wore their own kinds of clothes. No matter how different these garments looked from one another, they were usually made from local materials and included signs and symbols identifying wealth, rank, and beliefs.

An Aztec Eagle Knight is dressed for battle.

Strict Control

Among the Aztecs of Meso-America, the right to wear different styles of clothing was strictly controlled. Unmarried girls left their hair loose. Married women wore braids with the ends pointing up like horns. Only noblemen were allowed to wear cloaks reaching below the knee. The best, most courageous soldiers — known as "Eagle Knights" and "Jaguar Knights" — wore magnificent uniforms fashioned from real feathers and wild animal skins.

Signs of Distinction

In North America, high-ranking chiefs, warriors, and shamans wore clothes that displayed their high status. For practical reasons, these people wore the same basic clothing as ordinary men and women —

For religious rituals, Native people wore animal disguises, paint, and masks.

typically a robe or tunic and pants of deerskin (common among northern Native nations) or patterned woven blankets and wraps (usual among western desert peoples). High-ranking people added fur, feathers, beaks, shells, teeth, and bones as signs of their special ranks.

18

Puritan men who settled in
North America wore wool
or linen shirts, fitted jackets,
and knee-breeches.

Religious Symbols

Many of the first Europeans to settle in North America migrated there for religious reasons. They wanted freedom to live and worship in the ways they thought best. From the 1620s onward, their clothes were based on styles worn by other Puritans (religious reformers) in Europe. They favored plain, simple, modest clothing in dark colors, without fancy trimmings such as frills, lace, or embroidery. Over time, clothing evolved to suit North America's harsh climate. These new clothes included hard-wearing **buckskin** boots and jerkins (close-fitting, hip-length, collarless jackets). For warmth, they wore fur-lined hats and cloaks.

500 – 1750

Who else, apart from Aztec nobles, were allowed to wear long cloaks?

Conquistadors

From the early sixteenth through the eighteenth centuries, rival Europeans battled for control of the Americas. In Mexico, Spanish forces led by Hernán Cortés landed in central Mexico in 1519. They fought and conquered the native Aztec people in the space of just two years. Their protective clothing helped them as much as their weapons. While the native Aztecs dressed in clothing designed for symbolic, spiritual help, the Spanish conquistadors were clad in iron armor for protection. In Peru, Spanish forces, dressed in metal armor and led by Francisco Pizarro, quickly overcame the cloth-clad Inca forces.

Spanish forces wearing iron armor battle against cloth-clad Aztec forces in Mexico.

By about 1500, kings, popes, and other important people in Europe were beginning to give their servants uniforms rather than simple surcoats or heraldic badges. At the same time, certain colors — especially red and black — were increasingly linked with particular professions.

The Yeomen of the Guard (now nicknamed "Beefeaters") still wear uniforms based on Tudor designs.

Swiss Guards and Beefeaters

Since Roman times, European rulers had recruited troops of elite soldiers to guard themselves, their palaces, and their families. By about 1500, many royal bodyguards were wearing specially designed uniforms. In Italy, the Swiss Guards, who protected the Pope, wore striped tunics and **breeches** of red and gold. In England, the Yeoman of the Guard (founded in 1485 to protect King Henry VII at his coronation), also wore red uniforms, with a gold cipher (heraldic pattern) on the fronts of their tunics. This cipher represented the ruling monarch's initials.

Scholarly and Serious

In the sixteenth and seventeenth centuries, religious reformers known as Protestants said that the Catholic church had become too interested in money and possessions. They called for a return to simple ways of living and worshipping. To reflect these ideas, Protestant preachers chose simple black robes similar to those worn by students and scholars.

This portrait of the Protestant reformer Martin Luther, dressed in black, dates from the sixteenth century.

In Disguise

Catholic countries in southern Europe continued to celebrate traditional church festivals with special

Masked partygoers dance in the streets to the exciting beat of the carnival drum (*played by a musician, far right*).

entertainment. To mark the start of Lent, the fasting period before Easter, they held feasts and parties, called carnivals. At carnival time, merrymakers wore uniforms that included masks and costumes so that no one could tell who they were or criticize them for bad behavior. Carnival masks became a kind of unofficial uniform. It was almost unthinkable to attend a carnival party without one.

What does the word *carnival* mean?

National Identity

After about 1700, most professional soldiers had some kind of official uniform. Volunteers, however, wore their own clothing to war. They displayed loyalty to their side by wearing colored scarves or bunches of local plants or oak leaves pinned to their clothes. Local clothing was also chosen by rebels as a symbol of defiance against the ruling country. In Scotland, for example, Jacobite rebels fought against the Hanoverian dynasty (who ruled Britain from 1714 to 1837). Ordinary Jacobite soldiers wore their local dress — a kilt and plaid (a length of fabric draped like a cloak). So did the Scottish nobles who led them.

This portrait shows William Cumming wearing a kilt in 1714.

Western World 1750–1900

The late eighteenth and nineteenth centuries are often called a "golden age" of army and navy uniforms. For officers and many enlisted men, uniform clothes were more elaborate, colorful, and varied than ever before.

Naval Discipline

Naval uniforms clearly displayed the wearer's rank. In Britain, for example, crewmen wore natural beige woolen or linen shirts with wide, "bell-bottom" pants; officers wore navy-blue jackets with tight, white knee breeches (pants extending down to or just below the knee). Senior officers' jackets were decorated with **epaulettes** (a fringed strap worn on military uniforms), gold braid, plus badges won for bravery. Crewmen were usually bare-headed; officers wore tall hats with **rosettes** (badges made of ribbon or silk) or bunches of feathers.

This ornament was made to mark the victory of Nelson at Trafalgar. It shows some of the typical naval uniforms of the period.

Thin Red Line

Uniforms worn by soldiers were based on late eighteenth-century fashions — tight knee breeches (later replaced by long tight pants) plus close-fitting tunics that ended at the waist or reached to the thigh. Each country and regiment had its own special tunic, colors, and styles. Russian troops wore green. North Germans wore "Prussian" blue. Swedes wore blue and yellow. Because of their blood-colored tunics, British troops were nicknamed "Redcoats."

This Civil War Confederate jacket and pants belonged to a member of the Twentieth Georgia Infantry in 1864.

A man from the Thameside Aviation Museum in England models a Victorian fireman's uniform.

Civil Defense

As cities grew larger and more densely populated in the nineteenth century, they needed better protection from natural disasters and crime. Police forces and fire departments were newly founded or reorganized. So that the public would recognize, trust, and respect them, they were issued uniforms in military styles.

Who invented bell-bottom pants, and why?

Uniforms at Home

Although new nineteenth-century industries and inventions created jobs and made profits, a very large gap remained between rich and poor. Wealthy families could afford to employ large numbers of domestic servants to cook, clean, care for children, wait on tables, run messages, drive horse-drawn carriages, and receive visitors at their homes. Male and female servants were expected to be clean, neat, and well dressed. Employers issued them with uniforms once or twice a year. Servants had to wear the clothes that they were given, however awkward or uncomfortable they were.

A Victorian maid sits down to rest in *Her First Place*, by George Dunlop Leslie.

Western World 1900–1950

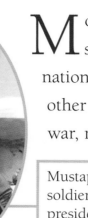

Mustapha Kemal, a soldier and later the president of Turkey, wears khakis here.

Most of the years of the early twentieth century were scarred by wars. Millions of soldiers from many nations died fighting in World War I (1914–1918) and in other smaller wars that followed. To fill in for the men at war, millions of women began to work outside the home.

Khakis

Until 1914, many armies still issued bright-colored uniforms to their men. After that, improved weapons, such as accurate rifles, and better optical devices, such as binoculars, made bright uniforms easy to hit at long range. In 1902, British and United States armies introduced new, less noticeable uniforms. These were based on greenish-brown clothes called khakis worn by late nineteenth-century British troops in India and Africa. Khakis soon became standard issue for armies.

Out to Work

Many women were widowed during World War I. Many single women were left with little chance of marrying. They all had to go out to work to support themselves. Women often had to take poor-paying jobs because of male prejudice and their own lack of training. For some jobs, such as waitressing, a uniform was a sign of low rank. For other jobs, such as nursing and teaching, the uniform was a proud statement of skilled status.

A waitress serves tea in a London restaurant in 1920.

Clothes for School

By about 1900, education was compulsory in many Western nations. In much of Europe, the school uniform was a long-sleeved smock worn over everyday clothes. In Britain, uniforms were more elaborate, even for poor pupils. By the 1920s, boys had to wear baggy shorts (usually gray), woolen socks, shirts with collars, school ties, caps with

Sports clothes and school uniforms were often closely linked. Children's blazers and gym clothes were copied from adult sportswear. These hockey players were photographed in 1946 in Wales.

badges, and often a blazer jacket. Girls also had to wear men's-style shirts and ties, knee-length woolen "gym-slips," blazers, and long knitted stockings.

Camouflage and Skirts

*What does the name **khaki** mean?*

In 1939, World War II was declared. It lasted until 1945. Fighting men on both sides wore new kinds of uniforms, including camouflage (patterns that helped soldiers hide in fields and woods) and battle dress (loose pants, fastened at the ankle) plus a bloused, long-sleeved top. For the first time, large numbers of women joined both the armed forces and civilian defense teams. They all wore specially designed uniforms based on men's styles. Except for those in a few specialized jobs, such as auto repairs, pants for women were banned.

Like men, women who joined the U.S. Air Force during World War II wore garrison caps as part of their uniform.

Western World 1950–2000

Late twentieth-century uniforms were a mixture of traditional and modern. Whether for peaceful tasks or for war, they fulfilled the same needs as earlier uniforms. They were often made from new, artificial fibers and worn by people doing newly created jobs.

Chinese Communist Party leader Mao Zedong (1893-1976) wears a Mao suit, a fashion he imposed on the general Chinese population.

Uniforms for the People

Many twentieth-century wars were fought on difficult terrain — from dense jungle to desert sands. These challenging environments required advanced military clothing. In 1995, the first computer-generated camouflage patterns were pioneered by Canadian scientists. In other nations, old-style uniforms still had a powerful impact. In China during the Cultural Revolution (1966–1976), troops of Red Guards (young Communists) forced the vast Chinese population to wear two-piece "Mao-suit" uniforms as a sign that they accepted extreme Red Guard policies.

Football players wear helmets, cleats, skin-tight, stretchy pants, and shirts big enough to cover their shoulder pads.

Sports Can Sell

Beginning in 1950, sports became big business. Sports clothes became a fast-growing part of the global clothing industry. Eye-catching uniforms strengthened a team's image and created profitable opportunities for selling similar clothes to fans. Streamlined, functional clothes made of new elastic fibers helped improve sports performance for

professionals and amateurs alike. Sports
styles can boost people's morale. Many who wear
athletic clothes feel more athletic and healthy.

Teamwork

New products and ways of working led to new
types of uniforms. In the 1980s and 1990s,
Japanese factories pioneered new, team-based
techniques for producing electrical goods and
motor vehicles. Team members were loyal to
each other and to their company. They often
wore company uniforms that were light and
comfortable. These uniforms encouraged their
team spirit. In other high-tech factories, goods

In 1995, Japanese team
workers in a factory in
Tokyo wore overalls.

1950 – 2000

had to be made in dust-free environments. Workers began to be issued
special uniforms that covered most of the body, including the hair. All
these workers were valued for their skills, hard work, and dedication.
In their uniforms, though, many looked almost like robots or machines.

This British traffic
warden's uniform is
similar to that of a
British police officer's.

Motor Services

Changes in society, such as widespread car
ownership, created many new jobs and new
demands for uniforms. Highway sheriffs, road
accident and ambulance crews, and traffic police
all now wear distinctive clothes. These uniforms
help identify them as they patrol the streets and
highways. Uniforms also help enforce a person's
authority when he or she is dealing with people
who might be injured, shocked, or hostile.

Global Styles Today

A U.S. officer poses with the Interceptor body armor, or small-arms protective inserts.

Today, just as thousands of years ago, uniforms are used to create a sense of belonging. Technology has resulted in ever more sophisticated uniforms, while traditional dress codes are making a new impact. Fashionable shoppers are creating their own "uniforms" by purchasing clothes that look like those of all the other people in their chosen group.

Better Performance

Designers of military uniforms aim to make clothes that will perform well under pressure. Most new uniforms, such as the U.S. Army Combat Uniform (ACU), feature loose shirts worn over wide trousers. Garments are made of mixed green, gray, and tan camouflage cloth. They have Velcro® tabs to fasten name tags showing the wearer's name, rank, and duties. Built-in **infrared** squares allow wearers to be identified in the dark.

Riot Gear

Under fire, soldiers, police, and security guards wear body armor. Armor protects, hides individual identity, and helps these people appear as part of a formidable team. Some new armor makes use of ancient designs, such as the metal ridge at the back of the neck first seen on Roman helmets. It also features modern manufactured materials, such as transparent plastic and shock-absorbing foam.

A U.S. soldier wears the latest Army Combat Uniform (ACU) in 2005.

The *khimar* (head scarf) is part of modest Muslim dress.

Religion and Politics

Today, as in the past, clothes can make a religious or political statement. For example, governments and religious leaders in some Muslim countries encourage male and female citizens to put on *hijab* (modest dress). To them, wearing Muslim "uniform" styles, such as the all-covering *abayah* (cloak), is one way for Muslims to practice their faith. These clothes can also be used as a method of enforcing religious or political conformity among people.

What do U.S. military wear under their ACU?

Worldwide Style

Today's media technologies mean that news about clothes and fashions can spread quickly all over the world. Different social groups choose their own styles of clothing. Advertising and peer pressure can make these group styles close to a uniform. Actual uniforms, however, are now required less often than in the past. For many, the "uniform" of jeans and a top connects people to a worldwide community.

Today, even though most Western people have more time, freedom, and money to choose a variety of clothing styles, many still like to wear simple, care-free "uniforms," such as jeans and T-shirts.

Glossary

Berserkers Viking warriors who wore bearskin shirts and fought furiously

breeches short, tight pants

buckskin deer skin

candidates people who run for election to public office

cataracts waterfalls such as those on the Nile River in Egypt in North Africa

chain mail body protection made from linked metal rings.

city-states cities that rule themselves and the surrounding land

crook a hooked stick, often used by shepherds to herd their sheep

epaulettes shoulder protectors or decorations, often used on military uniforms

flail a heavy rod or stick, often hung with a shorter stick or sticks, that is used to beat the chaff from grain, herd animals, or show authority

habits plain, sober uniform clothes worn by monks, nuns, and friars and usually styled to show that the wearers are members of a specific religious order

hoplites citizen foot soldiers, usually heavily armed, of ancient Greece

infrared rays of energy given out by hot objects, including the Sun, that cannot be seen but can be felt

kilts short, knee-length skirts worn by men, usually pleated or folded in front

meditating entering a peaceful state of mind, usually by sitting quietly and repeating a special word or phrase

Mesopotamian having to do with the land in the Middle East between the Tigris and Euphrates Rivers that is now part of Iraq

nemes an Egyptian head-covering made of cloth

plate armor body protection made of carefully shaped pieces of metal

rank the place or position a person has compared to others in the group to which the person belongs

rosettes circular decorations made of ribbon or braid

saffron a deep orange dye made from crocus flowers

senate the ruling council in ancient Rome

shamans people believed to use magic to heal

surcoats loose cloth robes worn on top of armor

Sufi having to do with a Muslim spiritual movement in which members dance to try to connect with God

talismans lucky charms; objects believed to have magic powers

terra-cotta baked clay either glazed or unglazed

tunics simple slip-on clothes that are knee-length or longer and usually belted

Answers

Page 5: in 1863, by Swiss philanthropist Henri Dunant

Page 7: most of them were killed in battle because their magic shirts were no protection against bullets

Page 9: probably because being stung by real Egyptian flying insects could be serious

Page 10: athletes ran wearing nothing at all!

Page 13: coarse, rough, scratchy sackcloth because it made them suffer plus a sprinkling of ashes to symbolize death and decay.

Page 15: the workers who designed and built his tomb and who laid his body to rest there when he died

Page 17: plain, white, handwoven cloth. This tradition may have had links with ancient Egyptian customs.

Page 19: ordinary soldiers whose legs had been scarred in battle

Page 21: "Goodbye to meat," because believers had to give up meat and other favorite foods during Lent.

Page 23: U.S. sailors, in about 1800, so that they could pull their pants on quickly over their shoes.

Page 25: It is based on a Hindi (Indian) word meaning "dust-colored."

Page 27: The first artificial fibers were easy to wash and shed creases, but they could be hot and unhealthy to wear because they did not "breathe." Artificial fibers had to be improved before they were comfortable enough to be practical.

Page 29: moisture-absorbing T-shirt, underwear, and socks, all made from high-tech artificial fibers

Index